Maddy oconnor

Flower Fairies of the Summer

POEMS AND PICTURES BY

CICELY MARY BARKER

BLACKIE: LONDON AND GLASGOW

SPRING GOES, SUMMER COMES

The little darling, Spring,
      Has run away;
The sunshine grew too hot for her to stay.

She kissed her sister, Summer,
      And she said:
" When I am gone, you must be queen
      instead."

Now reigns the Lady Summer,
      Round whose feet
A thousand fairies flock with blossoms sweet.

Blackie & Son Ltd., 5 Fitzhardinge Street London, W.1
Bishopbriggs, Glasgow

Printed in Great Britain by Smith and Ritchie Ltd., Edinburgh

CONTENTS

THE SONG OF
THE BUTTERCUP FAIRY

'Tis I whom children love the best;
   My wealth is all for them;
For them is set each glossy cup
   Upon each sturdy stem.

O little playmates whom I love!
   The sky is summer-blue,
And meadows full of buttercups
   Are spread abroad for you.

The Buttercup Fairy

THE SONG OF
THE HERB ROBERT FAIRY

Little Herb Robert,
   Bright and small,
Peeps from the bank
   Or the old stone wall.

Little Herb Robert,
   His leaf turns red;
He's wild geranium,
   So it is said.

The Herb Robert Fairy

THE SONG OF
THE SORREL FAIRY

Like ladies clad in gold and white
  The ox-eye daisies stand;
And by them riseth up the height
  Of Sorrel near at hand,
Who keepeth watch like trusty knight
  Throughout the meadow-land.

O coral red of Sorrel's head!
  O banner that I hold
Above the meadow-grass outspread
  And daisies white and gold,
Until my dangling seeds are shed,
  And summer groweth old!

The Sorrel Fairy

THE SONG OF
THE FORGET-ME-NOT FAIRY

So small, so blue, in grassy places
    My flowers raise
    Their tiny faces.

By streams my bigger sisters grow,
    And smile in gardens,
    In a row.

I've never seen a garden plot;
    But though I'm small,
    Forget me not!

The Forget-me-not Fairy

THE SONG OF
THE POPPY FAIRY

The green wheat's a-growing,
  The lark sings on high;
In scarlet silk a-glowing,
  Here stand I.

The wheat's turning yellow,
  Ripening for sheaves;
I hear the little fellow
  Who scares the bird-thieves.

Now the harvest's ended,
  The wheat-field is bare;
But still, red and splendid,
  I am there.

The Poppy Fairy

THE SONG OF
THE FOXGLOVE FAIRY

" Foxglove, Foxglove,
  What do you see?"
The cool green woodland,
  The fat velvet bee:
Hey, Mr. Bumble,
  I've honey here for thee!

" Foxglove, Foxglove,
  What see you now?"
The soft summer moonlight
  On bracken, grass, and bough;
And all the fairies dancing
  As only they know how.

The Foxglove Fairy

THE SONG OF
THE WILD ROSE FAIRY

I am the queen whom everybody knows:
      I am the English Rose;
As light and free as any Jenny Wren,
      As dear to Englishmen;
As joyous as a Robin Redbreast's tune,
      I scent the air of June;
My buds are rosy as a baby's cheek;
      I have one word to speak,
One word which is my secret and my song,
'Tis " England, England, England " all day
    long.

The Convolvulus Fairy

THE SONG OF
THE WHITE CLOVER FAIRY

I'm little White Clover, kind and clean;
Look at my threefold leaves so green;
Hark to the buzzing of hungry bees:
" Give us your honey, Clover, please!"

Yes, little bees, and welcome, too!
My honey is good, and meant for you!

The White Clover Fairy

THE SONG OF
THE HONEYSUCKLE FAIRY

The lane is deep, the bank is steep,
   The tangled hedge is high;
And clinging, twisting, up I creep,
   And climb towards the sky.
O Honeysuckle, mounting high!
O Woodbine, climbing to the sky!

The people in the lane below
   Look up and see me there,
Where I my honey-trumpets blow,
   Whose sweetness fills the air.
O Honeysuckle, waving there!
O Woodbine, scenting all the air!

The Honeysuckle Fairy

THE SONG OF
THE BIRD'S-FOOT TREFOIL FAIRY

Here I dance in a dress like flames,
And laugh to think of my comical names.
Hoppetty hop, with nimble legs!
Some folks call me *Bacon and Eggs*!
While other people, it's really true,
Tell me I'm *Cuckoo's Stockings* too!
Over the hill I skip and prance;
I'm *Lady's Slipper*, and so I dance,
Not like a lady, grand and proud,
But to the grasshoppers' chirping loud.
My pods are shaped like a dicky's toes:
That is what *Bird's-Foot Trefoil* shows;
This is my name which grown-ups use,
But children may call me what they choose.

The Bird's-Foot Trefoil Fairy

THE SONG OF
THE NIGHTSHADE FAIRY

My name is Nightshade, also Bittersweet;
    Ah, little folk, be wise!
Hide you your hands behind you when we
    meet,
    Turn you away your eyes.
My flowers you shall not pick, nor berries eat,
    For in them poison lies.

(Though this is so poisonous, it is not the Deadly Nightshade, but the Woody Nightshade. The berries turn red a little
later on.)

The Nightshade Fairy

THE SONG OF
THE WHITE CAMPION FAIRY

The Lady Summer now doth reign
  In rich and queenly state,
And I among her royal train
  Within her meadows wait.
O little heed have I for fame,
  And little do I care
If few do know me by my name
  And none do call me rare.
No fairer sight, no purer white,
  Than this of mine is seen;
I stand in spotless livery
  And serve my Lady Queen.

The White Campion Fairy

THE SONG OF
THE HAREBELL FAIRY

O bells, on stems so thin and fine!
    No human ear
    Your sound can hear,
O lightly chiming bells of mine!

When dim and dewy twilight falls,
    Then comes the time
    When harebells chime
For fairy feasts and fairy balls.

They tinkle while the fairies play,
    With dance and song,
    The whole night long,
Till daybreak wakens, cold and grey,
And elfin music fades away.

(The Harebell is the Bluebell of Scotland.)

The Harebell Fairy

THE SONG OF
THE HEATHER FAIRY

" Ho, Heather, ho! From south to north
Spread now your royal purple forth!
Ho, jolly one! From east to west,
The moorland waiteth to be dressed!"

I come, I come! With footsteps sure
I run to clothe the waiting moor;
From heath to heath I leap and stride
To fling my bounty far and wide.

(The heather in the picture is bell heather, or heath; it is
different from the common heather which is also called ling.)

The Heather Fairy

THE SONG OF
THE YARROW FAIRY

Among the harebells and the grass,
  The grass all feathery with seed,
I dream, and see the people pass:
  They pay me little heed.

And yet the children (so I think)
  In spite of other flowers more dear,
Would miss my clusters white and pink,
  If I should disappear.

(The Yarrow has another name, Milfoil, which means
Thousand Leaf; because her leaves are all made up of very
many tiny little leaves.)

The Yarrow Fairy

THE SONG OF
THE TOADFLAX FAIRY

The children, the children, they call me funny
    names,
They take me for their darling and partner in
    their games;
They pinch my flowers' yellow mouths, to
    open them and close,
  Saying, *Snap-Dragon!*
      Toadflax!
          or, *darling Bunny-Nose!*

The Toadflax, the Toadflax, with lemon-
    coloured spikes,
With funny friendly faces that everybody
    likes,
Upon the grassy hillside and hedgerow bank
    it grows,
  And it's *Snap-Dragon!*
      Toadflax!
         and *darling Bunny-Nose!*

The Toadflax Fairy

THE SONG OF
THE SCABIOUS FAIRY

Like frilly cushions full of pins
For tiny dames and fairykins;

Or else like dancers decked with gems,
My flowers sway on slender stems.

They curtsey in the meadow grass,
And nod to butterflies who pass.

The Scabious Fairy

THE SONG OF
THE THISTLE FAIRY

I am the soldier of the field,
  All armed with swords and spears;
Beware the weapons which I wield,
  Unless you look for tears.

The prickles of my leaves and stem
  Can stab as needles do;
But, if you never handle them,
  They'll do no harm to you.

And presently my purple crown,
  Which looks so brave to-day,
Shall turn to softest thistle-down
  And lightly float away.

The Thistle Fairy

THE SONG OF
THE WILD THYME FAIRY

O people of the town,
Come seek me on the down,
The sunny open hill-top, wide and free,
Where the turf beneath your feet
Is good and clean and sweet,
The air is swept with breezes from the sea;
And you who breathe my scent,
Shall find your heart's content
For ever in the land of downs with me.

The Wild Thyme Fairy

THE SONG OF
THE SCARLET PIMPERNEL FAIRY

By the furrowed fields I lie,
Calling to the passers-by:
" If the weather you would tell,
Look at Scarlet Pimpernel."

When the day is warm and fine,
I unfold these flowers of mine;
Ah, but you must look for rain
When I shut them up again!

Weather-glasses on the walls
Hang in wealthy people's halls:
Though I lie where cart-wheels pass,
I'm the Poor Man's Weather-Glass!

The Scarlet Pimpernel Fairy

THE SONG OF
THE GREATER KNAPWEED FAIRY

Oh, please, little children, take note of my
    name:
To call me a thistle is really a shame:
I'm harmless old Knapweed, who grows on
    the chalk,
I never will prick you when out for your walk.

Yet I should be sorry, yes, sorry indeed,
To cut your small fingers and cause them to
    bleed;
So bid me Good Morning when out for your
    walk,
And mind how you pull at my very tough
    stalk.

(Sometimes this Knapweed is called Hardhead; and he has
a brother, the little Knapweed, whose flower is not quite like
this.)

The Greater Knapweed Fairy

THE SONG OF
THE TRAVELLER'S JOY FAIRY

Traveller, traveller, tramping by
To the seaport town where the big ships lie,
See, I have built a shady bower
To shelter you from the sun or shower.
Rest for a bit, then on, my boy!
Luck go with you, and Traveller's Joy!

Traveller, traveller, tramping home
From foreign places beyond the foam,
See, I have hung out a white festoon
To greet the lad with the dusty shoon.
Somewhere a lass looks out for a boy:
Luck be with you, and Traveller's Joy!

(Traveller's Joy is Wild Clematis; and when the flowers are over, it becomes a mass of silky fluff, and then we call it Old Man's Beard.)

The Traveller's Joy Fairy

THE SONG OF
THE RAGWORT FAIRY

Now is the prime of Summer past,
    Farewell she soon must say;
But yet my gold you may behold
    By every grassy way.

And what though Autumn comes apace,
    And brings a shorter day?
Still stand I here, your eyes to cheer,
    In gallant gold array.

The Ragwort Fairy